Congressional
Research
Service

Fatherhood Initiatives: Connecting Fathers to Their Children

Carmen Solomon-Fears
Specialist in Social Policy

December 7, 2012

Congressional Research Service

7-5700

www.crs.gov

RL31025

Summary

In 2012, 25% of families with children (under age 18) were maintained by mothers. According to some estimates, about 60% of children born during the 1990s spent a significant portion of their childhood in a home without their father. Research indicates that children raised in single-parent families are more likely than children raised in two-parent families (with both biological parents) to do poorly in school, have emotional and behavioral problems, become teenage parents, and have poverty-level incomes. In hopes of improving the long-term outlook for children in single-parent families, federal, state, and local governments, along with public and private organizations, are supporting programs and activities that promote the financial and personal responsibility of noncustodial fathers to their children and increase the participation of fathers in the lives of their children. These programs have come to be known as "responsible fatherhood" programs.

Sources of federal funding for fatherhood programs include the Temporary Assistance for Needy Families (TANF) program, TANF state Maintenance-of-Effort (MOE) funding, Child Support Enforcement (CSE) funds, and Social Services Block Grant (Title XX) funds.

In the 106th, 107th, and 108th Congresses, bills containing specific funding for responsible fatherhood initiatives were debated. President George W. Bush, a supporter of responsible fatherhood programs, included funding for such programs in each of his budgets. In the 109th Congress, P.L. 109-171 (the Deficit Reduction Act of 2005) was enacted. It included a provision that provided up to $50 million per year (FY2006-FY2010) in competitive grants to states, territories, Indian tribes and tribal organizations, and public and nonprofit community groups (including religious organizations) for responsible fatherhood initiatives. The Obama Administration's FY2011 budget included a proposal to substantially increase funding for responsible fatherhood programs under a proposed new Fatherhood, Marriage, and Families Innovation Fund. Under the proposal, the new fund would have received $500 million for FY2011 (this proposal was not passed by either the House or the Senate). Instead, P.L. 111-291 (enacted December 8, 2010) extended funding for the Title IV-A Healthy Marriage and Responsible Fatherhood grants for an additional year (i.e., through FY2011). For FY2011, it appropriated $75 million for awarding funds for healthy marriage promotion activities and $75 million for awarding funds for activities promoting responsible fatherhood. Pursuant to P.L. 112-78 (enacted December 23, 2011), the Healthy Marriage and Responsible Fatherhood grant programs were extended at their FY2011 funding level (on a pro rata basis) through February 29, 2012. Pursuant to P.L. 112-96 (enacted February 22, 2012), the Healthy Marriage and Responsible Fatherhood grant programs were extended (at their FY2011 funding level) through the end of FY2012 (on a pro rata basis). P.L. 112-175 (the government-wide continuing resolution enacted on September 28, 2012) extended funding (on a pro rata basis) for the Healthy Marriage and Responsible Fatherhood grant programs through March 2013 (the first six months of FY2013).

Most fatherhood programs include media campaigns that emphasize the importance of emotional, physical, psychological, and financial connections of fathers to their children. Most fatherhood programs include parenting education; responsible decision-making; mediation services for both parents; providing an understanding of the CSE program; conflict resolution, coping with stress, and problem-solving skills; peer support; and job-training opportunities (skills development, interviewing skills, job search, job-retention skills, job-advancement skills, etc.).

The federal government's support of fatherhood initiatives raises a wide array of issues. This report briefly examines the role of the CSE agency in fatherhood programs and discusses initiatives to promote and support father-child interaction outside the parents' relationship.

Contents

Introduction 1

What Are Fatherhood Initiatives? 3

Research and Evaluation 5

    MDRC Parents' Fair Share Demonstration Project 5

    Fragile Families and Child Wellbeing Study 6

    Office of Child Support Enforcement (OCSE) Responsible Fatherhood Programs 7

    Partners for Fragile Families Demonstration 8

    Responsible Fatherhood, Marriage, and Family Strengthening Grants for Incarcerated
        and Reentering Fathers and Their Partners 10

    Other Evaluations 11

Issues 11

    CSE System and Noncustodial Parents Often at Odds 12

    Noncustodial Father Involvement vs. Promotion of Marriage vs. Maintenance of
        Fragile Families 14

Appendixes

Appendix. Legislative History of Federally Funded Responsible Federal Fatherhood
    Programs 16

Contacts

Author Contact Information 22

Introduction

In 2012, 25% of families with children (under age 18) were maintained by mothers. In 2012, 32% of the 35.0 million families with children (under age 18) were maintained by one parent;[1] this figure is up from 10% in 1970. Most of the children in these single-parent families were being raised by their mothers; in 2012, 79% of single-parent families were mother-only families and 21% were father-only families.[2] According to some estimates, about 60% of children born during the 1990s spent a significant portion of their childhood in a home without their biological father. Research indicates that children raised in single-parent families are more likely than children raised in two-parent families (with both biological parents) to do poorly in school, have emotional and behavioral problems, become teenage parents, and have poverty-level incomes as adults.[3] Nonetheless, it is widely acknowledged that most of these mothers, despite the added stress of being a single parent, do a good job raising their children. That is, although children with absent fathers are at greater risk of having the aforementioned problems, most do not experience them. In hopes of improving the long-term outlook for children in single-parent families, federal, state, and local governments, along with public and private organizations, are supporting programs and activities that promote the financial and personal responsibility of noncustodial fathers to their children and reduce the incidence of father absence in the lives of children.

The third finding of the 1996 welfare reform law (P.L. 104-193) states: "Promotion of responsible fatherhood and motherhood is integral to successful child rearing and the well-being of children." Moreover, three of the four goals of the Temporary Assistance for Needy Families (TANF) program are consistent with the components of most fatherhood programs. The three fatherhood-related goals are ending welfare dependence by employment and marriage, reducing out-of-wedlock pregnancies, and encouraging the formation and maintenance of two-parent families. Thus, states may spend TANF and TANF state Maintenance-of-Effort (MOE) funds on fatherhood programs. Further, any services that are directed toward the goal of reducing nonmarital births or the goal of encouraging two-parent families are free of income eligibility rules.

With the exception of the federal Child Support Enforcement (CSE) program, fathers historically have been ignored with regard to their input or participation in welfare programs. Moreover, it was not until 1996 that Congress broadened its view to acknowledge the non-economic contributions that fathers make to their children by authorizing the use of CSE funds to promote access and visitation programs. With the enactment of the 1996 welfare reform law, which helped reduce the welfare rolls, increase the employment of low-income mothers, and strengthen the CSE program, Congress began focusing its attention on the emotional well-being of children.

---

[1] U.S. Census Bureau, Current Population Survey, Annual Social and Economic Supplement, America's Families and Living Arrangements: 2012, Table F2. Family Households, By Type, Age of Own Children, and Educational Attainment of Householder: 2012, Internet release date: November 2012. See http://www.census.gov/hhes/families/data/cps2012.html.

[2] Ibid.

[3] Sara McLanahan and Gary Sandefur, *Growing Up With a Single Parent: What Hurts, What Helps* (Cambridge, MA: Harvard University Press, 1994), see also L. Bumpass, "Children and Marital Disruption: A Replication and Update," *Demography*, vol. 21 (1984), pp. 71-82; Rebecca A. Maynard, ed., *Kids Having Kids: A Robin Hood Foundation Special Report on the Costs of Adolescent Childbearing* (New York, 1996). Also see Fragile Families Working Paper WP12-20-FF, *The Causal Effects of Father Absence*, by Sara McLanahan, Laura Tach, and Daniel Schneider, October 10, 2012.

Historically, Congress had treated visitation and child support as legally separate issues, with only child support enforcement activities under the purview of the federal government. The 1996 law authorized an annual $10 million entitlement of CSE funds to states to establish and operate access and visitation programs.[4]

During the 106th Congress, Representative Nancy Johnson, then chair of the Ways and Means Subcommittee on Human Resources, stated, "To take the next step in welfare reform we must find a way to help children by providing them with more than a working mother and sporadic child support." She noted that many low-income fathers have problems similar to those of mothers on welfare—

> *While fathers must fulfill their financial commitments, they must also fulfill their emotional commitments. Dads play indispensable roles that cannot be measured in dollars and cents: nurturer, mentor, disciplinarian, moral instructor, and skills coach, among other roles.*
>
> **Source:** Executive Office of the President, *A Blueprint for New Beginnings—A Responsible Budget for America's Priorities* (February 2001), chap. 12, p. 75. (Administration of President George W. Bush)

namely, they are likely to have dropped out of high school, to have little work experience, and to have significant barriers that lessen their ability to find and/or keep a job. She also asserted that in many cases these men are "dead broke" rather than "dead beats," and that the federal government should help these noncustodial fathers meet both their financial and emotional obligations to their children.[5]

During the 106th, 107th, and 108th Congresses, responsible fatherhood bills were passed by the House (part of welfare reauthorization legislation), but not by the Senate. During the 109th Congress, P.L. 109-171—the Deficit Reduction Act of 2005 (S. 1932/H.Rept. 109-362) was enacted on February 8, 2006. It included a provision (in Title IV-A of the Social Security Act) that provided up to $50 million per year (FY2006-FY2010) for competitive responsible fatherhood grants.[6]

P.L. 111-291 (enacted December 8, 2010) extended funding for Title IV-A responsible fatherhood grants through FY2011. For FY2011, it appropriated $75 million for awarding funds for activities promoting responsible fatherhood.

P.L. 112-78 (enacted December 23, 2011) provided funding for the Responsible Fatherhood Program (and the Healthy Marriage Program) through February 29, 2012. P.L. 112-96 (enacted February 22, 2012) provided funding for the Responsible Fatherhood Program (and the Healthy Marriage Program) through September 30, 2012 (i.e., through FY2012). FY2012 funding for the two programs amounted to $150 million for the year, with half of the funds ($75 million) for the

---

[4] The child access and visitation program (Section 391 of P.L. 104-193) funded the following activities in FY2008: mediation, counseling, parental education, development of parenting plans, visitation enforcement, monitored visitation, neutral drop-off and pickup, supervised visitation, and development of guidelines for visitation and custody. In FY2008, about 85,000 individuals received services. The most common services were parent education, mediation, parenting plans, and supervised visitation. Most states used a mix of services. Most of the service providers were Human Services Agencies. Individuals were referred to services by the courts, CSE or welfare agencies, and others, as well as by self-referral. Services were both mandatory and voluntary, as determined by the state. Source: U.S. Department of Health and Human Services, Administration for Children and Families, Office of Child Support Enforcement, *Child Access and Visitation Grants: State/Jurisdiction Profiles for FY2008* (Washington DC, March 8, 2010).

[5] U.S. Congress, House Ways and Means Subcommittee on Human Resources, "Hearing on Fatherhood Legislation," Statement of Chairman Nancy Johnson, 106th Congress, 1st Session (October 5, 1999), p. 4.

[6] It also included about $100 million per year (FY2006-FY2010) for competitive healthy marriage promotion grants.

Responsible Fatherhood program and the other half of the funds for the Healthy Marriage program.

P.L. 112-175 (the government-wide continuing resolution enacted on September 28, 2012) extended funding for the Healthy Marriage and Responsible Fatherhood grant programs (at $150 million per year on a pro rata basis, divided equally between the two programs) through March 2013 (the first six months of FY2013).

See the **Appendix** of this report for a detailed legislative history of federally funded responsible fatherhood programs.[7]

In addition to federal funds exlicitly provided for responsible fatherhood programs, there are several other potential sources of federal funding for fatherhood programs. They include the TANF program, TANF state MOE funding, CSE funds, and Social Services Block Grant (Title XX) funds. According to HHS, about half of all states use some TANF funds for responsible fatherhood programs. In addition, many private foundations are providing financial support for fatherhood programs.

As mentioned above, states can use TANF block grant funds and state MOE funds on programs or services that accomplish the broad purposes of the TANF program. These sources of funding are potentially the largest sources of funding for fatherhood initiatives. Pursuant to P.L. 112-175, the TANF block grant to states is currently funded through March 2013 at an annual level of $16.5 billion. In addition, the state funding or MOE requirement (at the 75% level) is about $10.4 billion annually.[8] The cash welfare caseload declined from a peak of 5.1 million Aid to Families with Dependent Children (AFDC) families in 1994 to 1.9 million TANF families in December 2011.[9] The 63% reduction in the cash welfare caseload, together with the fixed block grant funding, means funds that otherwise would have been spent for cash assistance are now available for other purposes. These other purposes could include fatherhood initiatives, which are allowable uses of TANF and state MOE funds. Moreover, fatherhood initiatives are not subject to the requirements that apply to spending for ongoing cash assistance such as work requirements and time limits.

What Are Fatherhood Initiatives?

The realization that one parent, especially a low-income parent, often cannot meet the financial needs of her or his children is not new. In 1975, Congress viewed the CSE program as a way to make noncustodial parents responsible for the financial support of their children. In more recent years, Congress has viewed the CSE program as the link that could enable single parents who are low-wage earners to become self-supporting. With the advent of welfare reform in 1996, Congress agreed that many noncustodial parents were in the same financial straits as the mothers of their children who were receiving cash welfare. Thus, the 1996 welfare reform law (P.L. 104-

---

[7] For a detailed history of the responsible fatherhood policy arena, see Kathleen Sylvester and Kathleen Reich, "Making Fathers Count: Assessing the Progress of Responsible Fatherhood Efforts," Annie E. Casey Foundation, 2002.

[8] For additional information, see CRS Report RL32748, *The Temporary Assistance for Needy Families (TANF) Block Grant: A Primer on TANF Financing and Federal Requirements*, by Gene Falk.

[9] See CRS Report RL32760, *The Temporary Assistance for Needy Families (TANF) Block Grant: Responses to Frequently Asked Questions*, by Gene Falk.

---

193) requires states to have laws under which the state has the authority to issue an order or request that a court or administrative process issue an order that requires noncustodial parents who were unable to pay their child support obligation for a child receiving TANF benefits to participate in TANF work activities. As noted earlier, the 1996 law also provided funding for states to develop programs that supported the noncustodial parent's right and responsibility to visit and interact with his or her children.

To help fathers and mothers meet their parental responsibilities, many policy analysts and observers support broad-based collaborative strategies that go beyond welfare and child support agencies and include schools, work programs, prison systems, churches, community organizations, and the health care system.

Although Congress has authorized federal funding specifically designated for responsible fatherhood programs, many states and localities, private organizations, and nonprofit agencies also operate responsible fatherhood programs. Most fatherhood programs include media campaigns that emphasize the importance of emotional, physical, psychological, and financial connections of fathers to their children. To counterbalance some of the procedural, psychological, emotional, and physical barriers to paternal involvement, most fatherhood programs include many of the following components:

- parenting education—a course that describes the responsibilities of parents to their children; it discusses the need for affection, gentle guidance, and financial support; the need to be a proud example and respectful of the child's mother; and the need to recognize developmentally appropriate behavior for children of different ages and respond appropriately to children's developmental needs;

- responsible decision-making (with regard to sexuality, establishment of paternity, and financial support);

- mentoring relationships with successful fathers and successful couples;

- mediation services (communicating with the other parent, supervised visitation, discipline of children, etc.);

- providing an understanding of the CSE program;

- conflict resolution, coping with stress, problem-solving skills;

- developing values in children, appropriate discipline, participation in child-rearing;

- understanding male-female relationships;

- peer support;

- practical tasks to stimulate involvement—discussing ways to increase parent-child interactions such as fixing dinner for children, taking children to the park, playing a game, helping children with schoolwork, listening to children's concerns, and setting firm limits on behavior; and

- job training opportunities (skills development, interviewing skills, job search, job-retention skills, job-advancement skills, etc.).

Although most people refer to programs that seek to help fathers initiate or maintain contact with their children and become emotionally involved in their lives as "fatherhood" programs, the programs generally are gender-neutral. Their underlying goal is participation of the noncustodial parent in the lives of his or her children.

Research and Evaluation

Research findings indicate that father absence affects outcomes for children in terms of schooling, emotional and behavioral maturity, labor force participation, and nonmarital childbearing. These findings hold when income is taken into account, so the negative effects of father absence are not limited to those created by reduced family income.[10]

Both advocates and critics of the CSE program agree that parents should be responsible for the economic and emotional well-being of their children. They agree that many low-income noncustodial parents are unable to meet their financial responsibility to their children and are barely able, or unable, to support themselves. They also agree that some noncustodial parents do not know how to be responsible parents because they were not taught that knowledge or were not exposed to enough positive role models that they could emulate. Below are several examples of demonstration programs that seek to, or sought to, help low-income men become responsible fathers by helping them to gain employment or job mobility and by teaching them life skills so that they might reconnect with their children in a positive sustained manner.

MDRC Parents' Fair Share Demonstration Project

The Parents' Fair Share (PFS) Demonstration was a large-scale scientifically-designed (with experimental and control groups) national demonstration project conducted from 1994-1996 that combined job training and placement, peer support groups, and other services with the goal of increasing the earnings and child support payments of unemployed noncustodial parents (generally fathers) of children on welfare, improving their parenting and communication skills, and providing an opportunity for them to participate more fully and effectively in the lives of their children.[11]

The final report on the PFS demonstration concluded that the program did not significantly increase employment or earnings among the full sample of PFS participants during the two years after they entered the program. However, the program did increase earnings among a subgroup of men who were characterized as "less employable" (i.e., those without a high school diploma and with little recent work experience).[12]

One of the reports noted the following as lessons learned from the PFS demonstration:

---

[10] *Meeting the Challenge: What the Federal Government Can Do to Support Responsible Fatherhood Efforts—A Report to the President* [...] (Washington, DC, January 2001), http://fatherhood.hhs.gov/guidance01.

[11] The Parents' Fair Share (PFS) demonstration was funded by a consortium of private foundations (the Pew Charitable Trusts, the Ford Foundation, the AT&T Foundation, the McKnight Foundation, and the Northwest Area Foundation) and federal agencies (the U.S. Department of Human Services and the U.S. Department of Labor).The PFS demonstration was conducted in seven cities: Dayton, OH; Grand Rapids, MI; Jacksonville, FL; Los Angeles, CA; Memphis, TN; Springfield, MA; and Trenton, NJ.

[12] John M. Martinez and Cynthia Miller, *Working and Earning: The Impact of Parents' Fair Share on Low-Income Fathers' Employment* (New York: MDRC, October 2000).

Low-income noncustodial fathers are a disadvantaged group. Many live on the edge of poverty and face severe barriers to finding jobs, while those who can find work typically hold low-wage or temporary jobs. Despite their low, irregular income, many of these fathers are quite involved in their children's lives and, when they can, provide financial and other kinds of support.... Some services, such as peer support proved to be very important and valuable to the men and became the focal point of the program. Other services, such as skill-building, were hard to implement because the providers had little experience working with such a disadvantaged group; it was difficult to find employers willing to hire the men, and the providers were not equipped to deal with the circumstances of men who often were simply trying to make it from one day to the next. Finally, we learned about the challenges of implementing a program like PFS, which involves the partnership of various agencies with different goals, and about the difficulty of recruiting low-income fathers into such a program.[13]

Some of the recommendations for future programs included structuring the program to encourage longer-term participation and to include job retention services; providing fathers who cannot find private sector employment with community service jobs; earmarking adequate funding for employment services, involving custodial mothers in the program, and providing fathers with legal services to help them gain visitation rights; and encouraging partnerships between CSE agencies and fatherhood programs.[14]

Fragile Families and Child Wellbeing Study

A "fragile" family consists of low-income children born outside of marriage whose two natural parents are working together to raise them—either by living together or through frequent visitation.

The Fragile Families and Child Wellbeing Study followed a group of 4,700 children who were born in 20 large U.S. cities.[15] The total sample size was 4,700 families, including 3,600 unmarried couples and 1,100 married couples. The data were intended to be representative of nonmarital births in each of the 20 cities and also representative of all nonmarital births in U.S. cities with populations over 200,000. Both parents were interviewed at the child's birth and again when the child was age one, two, and five. In addition, in-home assessments of the children and their home environments were performed when the children were ages three and five. The parent interviews provided information on attitudes, relationships, parenting behavior, demographic characteristics, health (mental and physical), economic and employment status, neighborhood characteristics, and public welfare program participation. The in-home interview collected information on children's cognitive and emotional development, health, and home environment. The study was expected to provide previously unavailable information on questions such as the following:

- What are the conditions and capabilities of new unwed parents, especially fathers? How many of these men hold steady jobs? How many want to be involved in raising their children?

---

[13] Cynthia Miller and Virginia Knox, *The Challenge of Helping Low-Income Fathers Support Their Children: Final Lessons from Parents' Fair Share* (New York: MDRC, November 2001), pp. v-vi.

[14] Ibid., p. v.

[15] The Fragile Families and Child Wellbeing Study is a joint effort by Princeton University's Center for Research on Child Wellbeing (CRCW) and Center for Health and Wellbeing, and Columbia University's Social Indicators Survey Center and National Center for Children and Families (NCCF).

- What is the nature of the relationship between unwed parents? How many couples are involved in stable, long-term relationships? How many expect to marry? How many experience high levels of conflict or domestic violence?

- What factors push new unwed parents together? What factors pull them apart? How do public policies affect parents' behaviors and living arrangements?

- What are the long-term consequences for parents, children, and society of new welfare regulations, stronger paternity establishment, and stricter child support enforcement? What roles do child care and health care policies play? How do these policies play out in different labor market environments?[16]

A 2007 report that examined data pertaining to the surveyed children at age five found that 16% of participant mothers were married to the father at the time of the five-year interview. Despite not marrying, about 40% of the parents were still romantically involved at the five-year interview. In cases where the couple were no longer romantically involved, 43% of the fathers had seen their children in the month previous to the interview. According to the report:

> Fatherhood programs, such as education, training, support services, and content addressing issues of shared parenting, may also be appropriate for many new unmarried fathers. Engaging parents in responsible fatherhood programs (and weaving these programs into marriage promotion curriculums) early in their child's life may also help new fathers develop important parenting skills crucial to their child's healthy development. These programs may help fathers establish and maintain positive connections with their child and encourage their active participation in raising their child.[17]

The Fragile Families and Child Wellbeing in Middle Childhood Study received a $17 million grant from the National Institute of Child Health and Human Development (NICHD) of the Department of Health and Human Services to field a nine-year follow-up. The purpose of this project was to combine the core telephone surveys, in-home study, and teacher surveys into one larger project. Data collection began in 2007 and continued through the spring of 2010.[18] Short summaries, based on data from the Fragile Families and Child Wellbeing Study, highlight recent research findings and suggest policy implications on issues related to child well-being and the social and economic circumstances faced by unwed parents.[19]

Office of Child Support Enforcement (OCSE) Responsible Fatherhood Programs

The federal Office of Child Support Enforcement (OCSE) provided $2.0 million to fund Responsible Fatherhood demonstrations under Section 1115 of the Social Security Act. The programs operated in eight states between September 1997 and December 2002. The following eight states received Section 1115 grants or waivers from OCSE/Administration for Children and

---

[16] Irwin Garfinkel and Sara McLanahan, "Fragile Families and Child Well-Being: A Survey of New Parents," *Focus* (University of Wisconsin-Madison, Institute for Research on Poverty), vol. 21, no. 1 (spring 2000), pp. 9-11.

[17] *Fragile Families Research Brief,* June 2007, Number 39. Parents' Relationship Status Five Years After a Non-Marital Birth. Princeton University and Columbia University.

[18] For more information on the Fragile Families and Child Wellbeing Study, see http://www.fragilefamilies.princeton.edu/about.asp.

[19] See the following webpage for more information: http://www.fragilefamilies.princeton.edu/briefs2.asp.

Families (ACF) to implement and test responsible fatherhood programs: California, Colorado, Maryland, Massachusetts, Missouri, New Hampshire, Washington, and Wisconsin. These projects attempted to improve the employment and earnings of underemployed and unemployed noncustodial parents, and to motivate them to become more financially and emotionally involved in the lives of their children. Although the projects shared common goals, they varied with respect to service components and service delivery. OCSE also provided about $500,000 for an evaluation of the demonstration projects.

An outcome report on the programs found that (1) low-income noncustodial fathers are a difficult population to recruit and serve; (2) many of the participants found jobs with the programs' help, but they were low-paying jobs and relatively few of the participants were able to increase earnings enough to meet their financial needs and those of their children; (3) child access problems were hard to define and resolve, and mediation should be used more extensively; (4) child support guidelines result in orders for low-income noncustodial parents that are unrealistically high; (5) CSE agencies should collaborate with fatherhood programs and pursue routine enforcement activities, as well as adopt policies and incentives that are responsive to low-income fathers; and (6) criminal history was the norm rather than the exception among the program participants, many participants faced ongoing alcohol and substance abuse problems, many did not have reliable transportation, and many lacked a court-ordered visitation arrangement.[20]

The outcome report also found that employment rates and earnings increased significantly, especially for noncustodial parents who were previously unemployed. In addition, child support compliance rates increased significantly, especially for those who had not been paying previously. Moreover, the report found that 27% of the fathers reported seeing their children more often after completion of the program.

Partners for Fragile Families Demonstration

HHS has an ongoing partnership with the private-sector initiative called Partners for Fragile Families (PFF). The Partners for Fragile Families Project is an initiative of the National Center for Strategic Nonprofit Planning and Community Leadership (NPCL), a nonprofit organization based in Washington, DC.

In March 2000, HHS approved state waivers for the three-year Partners for Fragile Families (PFF) Demonstration projects. The purpose of the demonstration projects was to develop new ways for CSE agencies and community-based nonprofit and faith-based organizations to work together to help young noncustodial fathers (ages 16 to 25—who had not yet established paternity and who had little or no involvement with the CSE program) obtain employment, health, and social services; make child support payments to their children; learn parenting skills; and work with the mothers of their children to build stronger parenting partnerships. The PFF demonstration operated from 2000 to 2003 in 13 projects in nine states.[21] The demonstration project sites were located in California, Colorado, Indiana, Maryland, Massachusetts, Minnesota,

---

[20] Jessica Pearson, Nancy Thoennes, and Lanae Davis, with Jane Venohr, David Price, and Tracy Griffith, *OCSE Responsible Fatherhood Programs: Client Characteristics and Program Outcomes* (Washington, DC: U.S. Department of Health and Human Services, Administration for Children and Families, Center for Policy Research and Policy Studies (HHS Contract No. 100-98-0015), September 2003).

[21] The Chicago, IL, project withdrew from the demonstration.

New York, Pennsylvania, and Wisconsin.[22] According to HHS, of the $9.7 million in federal funding budgeted for the projects, $7.1 million was spent. An additional $1.4 million was spent for an evaluation of the projects.

An evaluation of the implementation of the PFF projects included the following statement:

> Although the concept of PFF was unique when it was developed in 1996, by the time the demonstration was fully implemented, other responsible fatherhood programs had started in many communities nationwide. Independent of PFF, the child support enforcement system was already incorporating more "father-friendly" approaches to service delivery at about the same time PFF was in its developmental stages. The child support system had begun to absorb the lessons learned from earlier fatherhood initiatives (such as the Parents' Fair Share project and the Responsible Fatherhood Demonstration). By the time PFF was operational, some may have viewed it as less pioneering than when it was conceived several years earlier. In addition, the number of young fathers who had not established paternity for their children decreased in the mid- to late-1990s as a result of the success of in-hospital paternity establishment initiatives across the country that established paternity at the time of a child's birth. The pool of young fathers without paternity established for their children had diminished in the PFF sites by the time the projects were implemented.[23]

HHS also sponsored two other evaluations of the PFF demonstration projects. Both of the evaluations were conducted by the Urban Institute. One of the Urban Institute reports includes case studies of selected fathers and their families, and the other report provides an analysis of economic and child support outcomes. The outcomes report indicated mixed results. The Urban Institute conducted a process and outcome evaluation interviewing all service providers (including child support enforcement, community-based organizations, and partner agencies) and analyzing client data matched with administrative wage data before and after the PFF program. This evaluation did not have a control group. According to the report, employment rates for participants before and after the program were basically low and unchanged (about 58% of PFF participants were employed 6 months before the demonstration and 59% of PFF participants were employed 6-12 months after enrollment in the demonstration). Although quarterly earnings of PFF participants increased after enrollment in the demonstration, at the end of 12 months, participants generally had poverty-level incomes. In contrast, the report indicated that there was a substantial increase in child support orders. At enrollment, about 14% of PFF participants had a child support order, whereas two years after enrollment, 35% of PFF participants had a child support order. For those PFF participants who paid child support, the average child support payment was $1,569 for the first year after enrollment and $2,296 for the second year after enrollment. The report also noted that, on average, about five monthly child support payments were made in the first year after enrollment and about seven monthly payments were made in the second year after enrollment.[24]

---

[22] See http://fatherhood.hhs.gov/index.shtml and http://www.npcl.org/program/pff.htm.

[23] The Urban Institute. *The Implementation of the Partners for Fragile Families Demonstration Projects*, by Karin Martinson, John Trutko, Demetra Smith Nightingale, Pamela A. Holcomb, and Burst S. Barnow, June 2007. See http://aspe.hhs.gov/hsp/07/PFF/imp/.

[24] Karin Martinson, Demetra Smith Nightingale, Pamela Holcomb, Burt Barnow, and John Trutko, "Partners for Fragile Families Demonstration Projects: Employment and Child Support Outcomes and Trends," The Urban Institute, September 2007.

Responsible Fatherhood, Marriage, and Family Strengthening Grants for Incarcerated and Reentering Fathers and Their Partners

An HHS-sponsored evaluation of responsible fatherhood programs, called the National Evaluation of the Responsible Fatherhood, Marriage, and Family Strengthening Grants for Incarcerated and Reentering Fathers and Their Partners (MFS-IP), began in 2006. The evaluation is a multiyear (quasi-experimental) study that is expected to run from 2006 through 2013.[25]

The Evaluation of MFS-IP is part of the U.S. Department of Health and Human Services (HHS), Administration for Children and Families (ACF) initiative to support healthy marriage and responsible fatherhood. Thirteen grantees in 12 different states have received five-year grants from the Office of Family Assistance of ACF to implement multiple activities to support and sustain marriages and families of fathers during and after incarceration. Grantees may also provide support for reentering the family and community from prison, parenting support including visitation during incarceration, and education and employment services during and after incarceration. To evaluate the overall effectiveness of the 13 MFS-IP grantees, the Assistant Secretary for Planning and Evaluation (ASPE), awarded a contract to RTI to conduct an implementation evaluation as well as a multi-site, longitudinal, impact evaluation of selected grantees.[26]

According to an HHS Research Brief:

> The implementation experiences of the MFS-IP grantees can inform future efforts to build healthy relationship skills among families affected by incarceration. While incarcerated, many individuals are interested in improving themselves and their relationships with their partners, children, and other family members. Although not all incarcerated persons are married or in intimate relationships, healthy relationship skills broadly apply to many types of interpersonal relationships. As observed by several grantees, relationships such as parent-child, correctional officer-inmate, inmate-inmate, and employer-employee could be improved by healthy relationship skills training.
>
> The impact study component of the MFS-IP evaluation, concluding in 2015, will determine the effectiveness of relationship education and other MFS-IP program components in strengthening relationship quality and stability and facilitating successful community reentry. Research suggests that healthy relationships contribute to reentry success, yet little is known about how to improve relationship quality for couples affected by incarceration. Relationship education that builds healthy relationship skills could play an important role in relationship quality throughout incarceration and during the critical reentry period. Even for lengthy periods of incarceration, communication and conflict resolution skills could result in more supportive relationships, improved co-parenting, and increased familial contact—all of which could be beneficial upon the individual's eventual release.[27]

---

[25] U.S. Government Accountability Office, "Healthy Marriage and Responsible Fatherhood Initiative—Further Progress Is Needed in Developing a Risk-Based Monitoring Approach to Help HHS Improve Program Oversight," GAO-08-1002, September 2008. Also see National Responsible Fatherhood Clearinghouse, "What Works in Fatherhood Programs? Ten Lessons From Evidence-Based Practice," by Jacinta Bronte-Tinkew, Allison Horowitz, and Allison Metz, at http://www.fatherhood.gov.

[26] See the following webpage for additional information: http://aspe.hhs.gov/hsp/08/MFS-IP/index.shtml.

[27] U.S. Department of Health and Human Services, Office of the Assistant Secretary for Planning and Evaluation, ASPE Research Brief, *Strategies for Building Healthy Relationship Skills Among Couples Affected by Incarceration*, by Christine Lindquist, Tasseli McKay, and Anupa Bir of RTI International, March 2012, p. 12.

A final report on the impact of the program is expected in 2015 or 2016.

Other Evaluations

The Obama Administration supports evidence-based programs as a way to use limited resources more effectively. The 2011[28] application announcement for responsible fatherhood programs (in accordance with P.L. 111-291) indicated that as a condition of acceptance of a responsible fatherhood award, grantees are required to participate fully in HHS-sponsored evaluations. HHS is investing resources in multiple federal evaluations to document successes, challenges, and lessons from responsible fatherhood programs that will provide useful information to program operators and policymakers. The 2011 application announcement for responsible fatherhood programs required that grantees operate comprehensive responsible fatherhood programs that integrate robust economic stability services, healthy marriage activities, and activities designed to foster responsible parenting.[29]

Thus, even though the emphasis of the Obama Administration was on more robust programs that could demonstrate effectiveness, the 2011 application announcement indicated that preference was to be given to grantees that operated DRA responsible fatherhood programs. According to HHS, on October 3, 2011, 120 grantees were awarded responsible fatherhood grants pursuant to P.L. 111-291.The grants are three-year grants, scheduled to run through September 2014.

Issues

In the late 1990s when interest in federally funding responsible fatherhood programs first gained national attention, some women's rights groups, such as the National Women's Law Center and the National Organization for Women (NOW), were concerned that an emphasis on the importance of fathers could lead to undervaluing single-parent families maintained by mothers; that services for fathers might be at the expense of services for mothers; and that the "pro-fatherhood" discourse could give fathers' rights groups more leverage in challenging child custody, child support, and visitation arrangements. Although that underlying tension has not disappeared completely, then and now, it was thought that the policy debate on responsible fatherhood initiatives had to be based on the view that the welfare of fathers, mothers, and children were intertwined and interdependent. Many analysts asserted that otherwise the debate would be very divisive and unproductive.[30]

---

[28] The grant awards were effective beginning October 2011 and are scheduled to run for three consecutive years up through September 2014. They are made for a three-year project period; funding for years 2 through 3 is not competitive and depends upon satisfactory performance, availability of funds, and the best interest of the government.

[29] U.S. Department of Health and Human Services, Administration for Children and Families, Office of Family Assistance, Pathways to Responsible Fatherhood Grants, June 28, 2011, http://www.acf.hhs.gov/grants/open/foa/view/ HHS-2011-ACF-OFA-FK-0194. Also see Virginia Knox, Philip A. Cowan, Carolyn Pape Cowan, and Elana Bildner, "Policies That Strengthen Fatherhood and Family Relationships: What Do We Know and What Do We Need to Know?" MDRC, 2009.

[30] William J. Doherty, Edward F. Kouneski, and Martha Farrell Erickson, *Responsible Fathering: An Overview and Conceptual Framework—Final Report* (Washington, DC: U.S. Department of Health and Human Services, Administration for Children and Families, Center for Policy Research and Policy Studies (HHS-100-93-0012), September 1996).

Many issues are associated with the federal government's support of fatherhood initiatives. A few examples are: Is the goal of federal policy to promote and support the involvement of fathers in their children's lives regardless of the father's relationship with the children's mother? What if the father has children by more than one woman? What is the federal policy with regard to incarcerated parents and parents recently released from prison? Does the federal government support counseling, education, and supervised visitation for abusive fathers so that they can reconnect with their children?[31]

The discussion below examines two issues that will likely impact the success of congressional fatherhood initiatives. The first deals with the role of the CSE agency in responsible fatherhood programs. The CSE program has the potential to impact more children and for longer periods of time than most other federal programs. In many cases, the CSE program may interact with parents and children for 18 years and, in some cases for up to 30 years if the noncustodial parent owes past-due child support. Some analysts contend that since many noncustodial parents have a negative view of the CSE program, the use of the CSE program to recruit fathers does not bode well for the success of such programs. Most federally funded responsible fatherhood programs are currently provided through competitive grants that are available to community organizations and other groups that have experience in working with low-income men. Moreover, many of the responsible fatherhood bills introduced in recent Congresses included evaluation components.

The second issue examines father involvement in the context of the father's relationship with the child's mother. The second issue is based on the premise that formal marital relationships last longer and are more conducive to long-term interaction between fathers and children than other types of relationships.

CSE System and Noncustodial Parents Often at Odds

During the period from FY1978 to FY2011, child support payments collected by the CSE agencies increased from $1 billion to $27.3 billion. Moreover, the program has made significant improvements in other program measures as well, such as the number of parents located, paternities established, and child support orders established. Advocates of the CSE program say that this dramatic program performance is aside from the indirect and intangible benefits of the program, such as increased personal responsibility and welfare cost-avoidance. Critics of the CSE program contend that even with an unprecedented array of "big brother" enforcement tools such as license (professional, driver's, recreational) and passport revocation; seizure of banking accounts, retirement funds, and lottery winnings; and automatic income withholding from pay checks, the program still collects only 20% of child support obligations for which it has responsibility[32] and collects payments for only 57% of its caseload.

Although the CSE program has historically been the policy answer to the problem of father absence, because its focus until recently was exclusively on financial support, it has had the

---

[31] For additional information, see Maria Cancian, Daniel R. Meyer, and Eunhee Han, "Child Support: Responsible Fatherhood and the Quid Pro Quo," *The Annals of the American Academy of Political and Social Science*, vol. 635, no. 140, 2011.

[32] This percentage accounts for arrearages (past-due child support). If child support arrearages are not taken into account the percentage is 62%. In FY2011, $144.6 billion in child support obligations ($33.3 billion in current support and $111.3 billion in past-due support) was owed to families receiving CSE services, but only $28.5 billion was paid ($20.8 billion in current support and $7.7 billion in past-due support).

practical effect of alienating many low-income fathers who are unable to meet their child support obligations. Some policy analysts maintain that fathers are, in effect, devalued when their role in their children's lives is based solely on their cash contributions. They argue that public policies are needed to support the father's role as nurturer, disciplinarian, mentor, and moral instructor.[33]

Information obtained from noncustodial fathers for various surveys and studies consistently tells the same story. Not surprisingly, noncustodial parents, especially low-income fathers, prefer informal child support agreements between themselves and the child's mother wherein they contribute cash support when they can and provide noncash aid such as taking care of the children from time to time and buying food, clothing, presents, etc., as often as they can. Many noncustodial fathers maintain that the CSE system is dismissive of their financial condition and continues to pursue child support payments (current support as well as arrearages) even when it knows that many of them can barely support themselves. They argue that for welfare families, the CSE program generally does not improve their child's well-being because their child support payments are used to benefit the state and federal government (i.e., welfare reimbursement) rather than their child. They contend that the CSE program causes conflicts between them and their child's mother because the women often use it as leverage by threatening to report them to CSE authorities, take them back to court, have more of their wages garnished, or have them arrested.[34]

Many observers maintain that noncustodial parents and the CSE program have irreconcilable differences and that the most that should be expected is for the noncustodial parent to clearly understand the purposes of the CSE program, the requirements imposed on the custodial parent, the noncustodial parents' rights to have their child support payments modified if they incur a financial change in circumstances, and that they as noncustodial parents have a moral and societal responsibility to have (or build) a loving relationship with their children.[35] If the CSE program continues to be the entrance to fatherhood programs (even in a recruitment capacity), most observers contend that the fact that the CSE program has not been effective in gaining the cooperation and trust of many noncustodial parents must be acknowledged and addressed. Several analysts suggest that to be successful, fatherhood programs may need to operate independently of the formal CSE system.

Others assert that more than any other agency of state government, the CSE program has the responsibility and is in the position to reach out to fathers who need supportive services. They point out that CSE agencies are already involved in forging relationships with fathers through partnerships with community-based organizations. They also note that CSE agencies provide a natural link to coordinate with TANF agencies to help families achieve self-sufficiency.[36]

---

[33] Wade F. Horn and Isabel V. Sawhill, *Making Room for Daddy: Fathers, Marriage, and Welfare Reform,* Brookings Institution Working Paper (Washington, DC, April 26, 2001), p. 4.

[34] Maureen Waller and Robert Plotnick, "A Failed Relationship? Low-Income Families and the Child Support Enforcement System," *Focus* (University of Wisconsin-Madison. Institute for Research on Poverty), vol. 21, no. 1 (spring 2000), pp. 12-17. See also *Family Ties: Improving Paternity Establishment Practices and Procedures for Low-Income Mothers, Fathers and Children* (Washington, DC: National Women's Law Center and Center on Fathers, Families, and Public Policy, 2000), pp. 9-11. Also see Fragile Families Research Brief 15 (Princeton University: Bendheim-Thoman Center for Research on Child Wellbeing, *Child Support Enforcement and Fragile Families,* April 2003.

[35] Waller and Plotnick, "A Failed Relationship? Low-Income Families and the Child Support Enforcement System," *Focus* (University of Wisconsin-Madison, Institute for Research on Poverty), vol. 21, no. 1 (spring 2000), pp. 12-17.

[36] National Child Support Enforcement Association, *Resolution on Fatherhood Initiatives,* adopted by the NCSEA Board of Directors on July 29, 2000, http://www.ncsea.org/files/2000_fatherhood_resol-final.pdf.

Noncustodial Father Involvement vs. Promotion of Marriage vs. Maintenance of Fragile Families

The first finding included in the 1996 welfare reform law is that marriage is the foundation of a successful society. The second finding is that marriage is an essential institution of a successful society that promotes the interests of children.[37] However, some child welfare advocates argue that marriage is not necessarily the best alternative for all women and their children. It is generally agreed that single-parent families are a better alternative for children than living with an abusive father. Many observers caution that government must be careful about supporting programs that provide cash incentives to induce people to marry or that coerce people into marrying. They note the problems associated with child-bride marriages and the short-term and often unhappy nature of the so-called "shotgun" marriage. Others respond that many long-lasting marriages were based on financial alliances (e.g., to increase economic status, family wealth, status in the community, etc.). They also point out that most government programs are sensitive to the issues of domestic violence and include supports to prevent or end such actions.

Many young children live with both of their parents who are not married but who are cohabiting. Noting this, some analysts argue that coercive policies designed to promote certain types of family structures (e.g., nuclear families) at the expense of others may undermine nontraditional family relationships. They contend that more emphasis should be placed on trying to meet the needs of these fragile families to enable them to stay together for longer periods of time. They maintain that if these parents wanted to be married they would be married.[38] They also point out that because of the complexity of many family relationships, there are no easy answers. From their perspective, a single-focus policy, no matter whether it aims to support traditional family relationships or fragile families, can place children in less desirable situations. For instance, promoting marriage of biological parents may result in supporting situations where some children in the household have a stepparent if all the children are not from the same union. Similarly, promoting fragile families could also result in supporting situations where a biological parent is absent if all of the children in the household are not all from the same union.

Some pro-marriage analysts point out that about 65% of children born to cohabiting parents will see their parents separate before they reach age 12, compared to about 24% of those born to married parents.[39]

Some observers note that even with supports it is unlikely that fragile families (unmarried couple) will remain together as long as married families. Thus, they argue that the promotion of

---

[37] The majority of pre-TANF evaluations of welfare initiatives that examined family formation decisions found little, if any, impact of state policies on decisions to marry. One exception was an evaluation of the Minnesota Family Investment Program (MFIP). In this program, compared to those who were subject to the AFDC requirements, more single-parent participants subject to new policies under MFIP got married and fewer of the two-parent participants had divorced within three years after the program began.

[38] See "Is Marriage a Viable Objective for Fragile Families?" *Fragile Families Research Brief 9* (Princeton University: Bendheim-Thoman Center for Research on Child Wellbeing, July 2002).

[39] David Popenoe and Barbara Dafoe Whitehead, "Should We Live Together? What Young Adults Need to Know about Cohabitation before Marriage, A Comprehensive Review of Recent Research," Second Edition, 2002. See also the Institute for American Values and the National Marriage Project, the State of Our Union—Marriage in America 2011, *When Baby Makes Three: How Parenthood Makes Life Meaningful and How Marriage Makes Parenthood Bearable*, by Brad Wilcox & Elizabeth Marquardt, December 8, 2011, p. 11.

---

marriage should be incorporated into fatherhood programs if the goal is lifetime involvement of fathers in the lives of their children.

In contrast, fatherhood initiatives are sometimes viewed as incompatible with initiatives that encourage the formation and maintenance of two-parent families, and with initiatives that promote marriage. In fact, many observers argue that the focus should be the participation of fathers in their children's lives, regardless of the marital status of the parents. As mentioned earlier, the TANF law states that the second purpose of the block grant is to "end the dependence of needy parents on government benefits by promoting job preparation, work, and marriage." The fourth purpose of the TANF block grant is to "encourage the formation and maintenance of two-parent families." There was some discussion about whether the fourth purpose means married-couple families or just two parents who are involved in their children's lives, regardless of whether they are married or even living together. In late 1999, the Clinton Administration issued *A Guide on Funding for Children and Families* through the TANF program, which broadly interpreted two-parent families to mean not only married-couple families, but also never-married, separated, and divorced parents, whether living together or not. Thus, many states classify their fatherhood programs and programs that encourage visitation by noncustodial parents under the rubric of fulfilling the purposes of the TANF program.[40]

In addition, it should be noted that some research indicates that there may be a racial component in the marriage promotion versus fatherhood involvement debate. In 2011, 72.3% of black births were to unmarried women, whereas only 29.1% of white births were to unmarried women. Given this demographic reality of black and white families in the United States, the authors of the study[41] maintained that proposals that earmark five times as much money for marriage promotion as for responsible fatherhood promotion[42] seemed "racially insensitive." (Readers should note that P.L. 109-171 funded marriage promotion grants at twice the amount of responsible fatherhood grants, i.e., $100 million per year versus $50 million per year for the five fiscal years FY2006-FY2010.[43]) Pursuant to P.L. 111-291, beginning in FY2011, the funding for responsible fatherhood grants was made equal to that of marriage promotion grants.

---

[40] Wade Horn, "Wedding Bell Blues: Marriage and Welfare Reform," *Brookings Review,* summer 2001, pp. 40-41.

[41] Ronald B. Mincy and Chien-Chung Huang, *The M Word: The Rise and Fall of Interracial Coalitions on Fathers and Welfare Reform.* Bowling Green State University Working Paper 02-7 (February 25, 2002), pp. 1-5, 32.

[42] H.R. 4737, as passed by the House in the 107th Congress, authorized $100 million annually for five years for competitive matching grants that require a dollar-for-dollar match for marriage promotion activities, resulting in total funding of $200 million annually for five years. Further, an additional $100 million per year for five years was authorized for research and demonstration grants and technical assistance related to the healthy marriage promotion activities. In contrast, H.R. 4737 (107th Congress) authorized $20 million annually for five years for responsible fatherhood grants.

[43] In contrast, S. 1309 and H.R. 2979, which were introduced in the 111th Congress, would have equalized funding in the healthy marriage and responsible fatherhood programs; both programs would have been funded at $100 million per year for specific years.

Appendix. Legislative History of Federally Funded Responsible Federal Fatherhood Programs

Beginning with the 106th Congress and with each subsequent Congress, responsible fatherhood programs have received both presidential and Congressional attention.

106th Congress (1999-2000)

For FY2001, Congress appropriated $3 million for a nongovernmental national fatherhood organization named the National Fatherhood Initiative (P.L. 106-553), as well as an additional $500,000 for the National Fatherhood Initiative and $500,000 for another non-governmental organization called the Institute for Responsible Fatherhood and Family Revitalization (P.L. 106-554).

During the 106th Congress, President Clinton's FY2001 budget included $255 million for the first year of a proposed "Fathers Work/Families Win" initiative to help low-income noncustodial parents and low-income working families work and support their children. The "Fathers Work/Families Win" initiative would have been administered by the Department of Labor (DOL). The "Fathers Work" component ($125 million) would have been limited to noncustodial parents (primarily fathers) and the "Families Win" component ($130 million) would have been targeted more generally to low-income families. Neither the House nor Senate FY2001 appropriations bill (H.R. 4577, 106th Congress) for the Departments of Labor, Health and Human Services, and Education, and Related Agencies included funding for the Fathers Work/Families Win proposal.

In addition, during the 106th Congress, legislation that included funding for a nationwide responsible fatherhood grants program was twice passed by the House (but not acted on by the Senate). H.R. 3073, the proposed Fathers Count Act of 1999, and H.R. 4678, the proposed Child Support Distribution Act of 2000 would have authorized funding ($140 million over two years in H.R. 3073 and $140 million over four years in H.R. 4678) to establish a program (usually referred to as fatherhood initiatives) to make grants to public or private entities for projects designed to promote marriage, promote successful parenting and the involvement of fathers in the lives of their children, and help fathers improve their economic status by providing job-related services to them.

107th Congress (2001-2002)

From the beginning of his presidency, President George W. Bush indicated his support for responsible fatherhood initiatives. President Bush's FY2002 budget (issued in February 2001, 107th Congress) proposed $64 million in 2002 ($315 million over five years) to strengthen the role of fathers in the lives of families. This initiative would have provided competitive grants to faith-based and community organizations that help unemployed or low-income fathers and their families avoid or leave cash welfare, as well as to programs that promote successful parenting and strengthen marriage. President Bush's FY2003 budget proposed $20 million (for FY2003) for competitive grants to community and faith-based organizations for programs that help noncustodial fathers support their families to avoid or leave cash welfare, become more involved in their children's lives, and promote successful parenting and encourage and support healthy marriages and married fatherhood.

During the 107th Congress, several bills (H.R. 1300/S. 653, H.R. 1471, S. 685, S. 940/H.R. 1990, H.R. 2893, H.R. 3625, H.R. 4090[44], S. 2524, and H.R. 4737) that included fatherhood initiatives were introduced, but none were enacted.

The purposes of the fatherhood programs in the bills introduced generally were the same: fatherhood programs must be designed to promote marriage through counseling, mentoring, and other activities; promote successful parenting through counseling, providing information about good parenting practices including payment of child support, and other activities; and help noncustodial parents and their families avoid or leave cash welfare by providing work-first services, job training, subsidized employment, career-advancing education, and other activities. However, the structure of the fatherhood programs differed.

Although H.R. 4737, amended, was passed by the House on May 16, 2002 (H.Rept. 107-460, Part 1), and reported favorably in the nature of a substitute by the Senate Finance Committee (S.Rept. 107-221) on July 25, 2002, it was not passed by the full Senate.

108th Congress (2003-2004)

President Bush's FY2004 budget proposed $20 million annually (for FY2004-FY2008) for promotion and support of responsible fatherhood and healthy marriage. The FY2004 budget proposal also would have gradually increased the annual funding of the CSE access and visitation grant program from $10 million annually to $20 million annually by FY2007.

President Bush's FY2005 budget proposed $50 million (for FY2005) for 75 competitive grants to faith-based and community organizations, together with Indian tribes and tribal organizations, to encourage and help fathers to support their families, avoid welfare, and improve their ability to manage family business affairs, and to support healthy marriages and married fatherhood.

During the 108th Congress several bills that included responsible fatherhood provisions (S. 5, S. 448, S. 604, S. 657, S. 1443, and S. 2830; H.R. 4 and H.R. 936) were introduced. None of the bills became law.

On February 13, 2003, the House passed H.R. 4 (108th Congress), a welfare reauthorization bill (that was essentially identical to H.R. 4737 as passed by the House in 2002) that would have provided $20 million per year for each of FY2004-FY2008 for a responsible fatherhood grant program.

On September 10, 2003, the Senate Finance Committee approved its version of H.R. 4 (S.Rept. 108-162), which would have established a $75 million responsible fatherhood program composed of four components for each of FY2004-FY2008: (1) a $20 million grant program for up to 10 eligible states to conduct demonstration programs; (2) a $30 million grant for eligible entities to

---

[44] H.R. 4090, as amended, was ordered reported by the House Ways and Means Committee on May 2, 2002 (H.Rept. 107-460, Part 1). The bill would have provided $20 million in grants per year for a five-year period (FY2003-FY2007) to public entities and nonprofit community entities, including religious organizations, and to Indian tribes and tribal organizations to promote responsible, caring, and effective parenting and to encourage positive father involvement, including the positive involvement of nonresident fathers; enhance the abilities and commitment of unemployed or low-income fathers to provide support for their families and to avoid or leave welfare; improve fathers' ability to effectively manage family business affairs; and encourage and support healthy marriages and married fatherhood. Note: H.R. 4737, a bill that included identical "fatherhood" provisions, passed the House on May 16, 2002.

conduct demonstration programs; (3) $5 million for a nationally recognized nonprofit fatherhood promotion organization to develop and promote a responsible fatherhood media campaign; and (4) a $20 million block grant for states to conduct responsible fatherhood media campaigns. Although H.R. 4 was debated on the Senate floor during the period March 29-April 1, 2004, consideration of the bill was not completed when a motion to limit debate on the bill failed to garner the necessary 60 votes. The Senate did not bring the bill back to the floor before the end of the session.[45]

109th Congress (2005-2006)

President Bush's FY2006 budget proposed $40 million (for FY2006) for a responsible fatherhood competitive grant program.

President Bush's FY2007 budget proposed $100 million for competitive matching grants to states for marriage promotion. It also included the $150 million for healthy marriage and responsible fatherhood programs that was included in P.L. 109-171 as part of welfare reauthorization. As noted in this report, pursuant to P.L. 109-171, $50 million is specifically allocated for responsible fatherhood programs.

During the 109th Congress several bills that included responsible fatherhood provisions were introduced. A couple of the bills were standalone bills that had been introduced in a previous Congress (S. 3607 and S. 3803) and some responsible fatherhood provisions were included in welfare reauthorization bills (H.R. 240/S. 105, S. 6, and S. 667). The Deficit Reduction Act of 2005 (S. 1932), which also included a provision that provided competitive grants for responsible fatherhood activities, was passed by Congress and enacted into law.[46]

Among other things, P.L. 109-171 reauthorized the TANF block grant at $16.5 billion annually through FY2010 and included a provision that provides up to $50 million per year (for each of FY2006-FY2010) in competitive grants to states, territories, Indian tribes and tribal organizations, and public and nonprofit community organizations, including religious organizations, for responsible fatherhood initiatives.

Under P.L. 109-171, responsible fatherhood funds could be spent on activities to promote responsible fatherhood through (1) marriage promotion (through counseling, mentoring, disseminating information about the advantages of marriage and two-parent involvement for children, etc.), (2) parenting activities (through counseling, mentoring, mediation, disseminating information about good parenting practices, etc.), (3) fostering economic stability of fathers (through work first services, job search, job training, subsidized employment, education, etc.), or (4) contracting with a nationally recognized nonprofit fatherhood promotion organization to develop, promote, or distribute a media campaign to encourage the appropriate involvement of

---

[45] During the period from 2002 to 2004, the responsible fatherhood bills that were passed by the House were part of welfare reauthorization legislation. (The funding for the Temporary Assistance for Needy Families (TANF) block grant, mandatory child care, and the abstinence education block grant—which were part of the 1996 welfare reform legislation (P.L. 104-193) whose funding authority expired on September 30, 2002—continued under a number of temporary extension measures.) Welfare reauthorization legislation was not enacted during this period.

[46] On December 19, 2005, the House passed the conference report on S. 1932, the Deficit Reduction Act of 2005 (H.Rept. 109-362). On December 21, the Senate passed the conference report on S. 1932 with amendments. The conference report was subsequently passed again by the House on February 1, 2006. On February 8, 2006, President Bush signed S. 1932 into P.L. 109-171.

parents in the lives of their children, focusing particularly on responsible fatherhood; and/or to develop a national clearinghouse to help states and communities in their efforts to promote and support marriage and responsible fatherhood.

110th Congress (2007-2008)

President Bush's FY2008 budget included the $150 million for healthy marriage and responsible fatherhood programs that was included in P.L. 109-171 as part of welfare reauthorization. As noted, pursuant to P.L. 109-171, $50 million is specifically allocated for responsible fatherhood programs for each of FY2006-FY2010.

Two bills that included responsible fatherhood provisions were introduced in the 110th Congress. S. 1626 was introduced by Senator Bayh, Senator Obama, and Senator Lincoln, and a House companion bill, H.R. 3395, was introduced by Representative Danny Davis (et al.). Among other things, S. 1626/H.R. 3395, the proposed Responsible Fatherhood and Healthy Families Act of 2007, would have increased funding for the responsible fatherhood grants (authorized by the Deficit Reduction Act of 2005, P.L. 109-171) to $100 million per year for each of FY2008-FY2010. (The total for the Healthy Marriage Promotion and Responsible Fatherhood grants would have increased from $150 million to $200 million per year for each of FY2008-FY2010.) The bills (S. 1626 and H.R. 3395) did not move out of committee.

111th Congress (2009-2010)

President Obama also is a supporter of responsible fatherhood programs. As a Senator, he was a cosponsor of a responsible fatherhood bill in both the 109th and 110th Congresses. As President, he has included in each of his budgets proposals to revise and fund responsible fatherhood programs.

The Obama Administration's FY2011 budget included a proposal to redirect funds from the Healthy Marriage and Responsible Fatherhood Programs ($150 million per year through FY2010; the responsible fatherhood portion is $50 million per year) to the proposed $500 million Fatherhood, Marriage, and Families Innovation Fund. The proposed Fatherhood, Marriage, and Families Innovation Fund would have been available for one year (FY2011) to provide three-year competitive grants to states.[47] According to one budget document, "The Fatherhood, Marriage, and Families Innovation Fund will serve as a catalyst for innovative service models that integrate a variety of service streams. The results from these demonstrations could form the basis for possible future TANF and CSE program changes at the federal or state level based on a multidimensional picture of the dynamics of family functioning and material self-sufficiency and child well-being."[48] The Fatherhood, Marriage, and Families Innovation Fund proposal was not passed by either the House or the Senate.

During the 111th Congress, three bills that included responsible fatherhood provisions were introduced. All three of the bills had been introduced in a previous Congress. None of the bills were passed by Congress.

---

[47] U.S. Department of Health And Human Services (ACF), "FY2011 Congressional Justification: Temporary Assistance for Needy Families (TANF)," pp. 304-305 http://www.acf.hhs.gov/programs/olab/budget/2011/TANF.pdf.

[48] Ibid.

S. 1309, the proposed Responsible Fatherhood and Healthy Families Act of 2009, was introduced on June 19, 2009, by Senators Bayh, Lincoln, and Burris. The House companion bill, H.R. 2979, was also introduced on June 19 by Representative Danny K. Davis (et al.). The House bill was referred to as the Julia Carson Responsible Fatherhood and Healthy Families Act of 2009. (These bills are almost identical to bills that were introduced in the 110th Congress.) The bills would have amended the TANF title of the Social Security Act (Title IV-A) to (1) increase funding for responsible fatherhood programs from $50 million per year to $100 million per year (for each of FY2008-FY2010); (2) expand procedures to address domestic violence; (3) expand activities promoting responsible fatherhood; (4) provide grants to healthy family partnerships for domestic violence prevention, for services for families and individuals affected by domestic violence, and for developing and implementing best practices to prevent domestic violence; and (5) eliminate the separate TANF work participation rate for two-parent families. The bills would have also made several changes to the CSE program (Title IV-D of the Social Security Act). It would have prohibited a state from collecting any amount owed to it by reason of costs it had incurred for the birth of a child for whom support rights have been assigned. They would have required a state to make a full distribution of collected child support to the family. They would have conditioned continued approval of a state plan under Title IV-D on state assessment of its policies with respect to barriers to employment and financial support of children. The bills also would have directed the HHS Secretary to award grants to states for an employment demonstration project involving a court- or state child support agency-supervised program for noncustodial parents so they can pay child support obligations. In addition, the bills would have directed the Secretary of Labor to award grants for transitional jobs programs and for public-private career pathways partnerships to help disadvantaged parents obtain employment.

S. 939, the proposed Protecting Adoption and Promoting Responsible Fatherhood Act of 2009, was introduced by Senator Landrieu on April 30, 2009. S. 939 would have required the HHS Secretary to establish an automated National Putative Father Registry. Among other things, S. 939 would have directed the Secretary to establish a nationwide responsible fatherhood and putative father registry educational campaign designed to (1) inform men about the National Putative Father Registry, the advantages of registering with a State Putative Father Registry, and the rights and responsibilities of putative fathers; and (2) inform women about the National Registry and its potential role in a pending or planned adoption or a termination of a putative father's rights. In addition, it would have required each state that desired to receive such a grant to develop and implement a state plan for promoting responsible fatherhood and permanency for children.

Pursuant to P.L. 111-291 (the Claims Resolution Act of 2010, enacted December 8, 2010), the responsible fatherhood program was extended for another year and its funding was increased from $50 million to $75 million. P.L. 111-291 extended funding for the Title IV-A Healthy Marriage and Responsible Fatherhood grants through FY2011. For FY2011, P.L. 111-291 appropriated $75 million for awarding funds for healthy marriage promotion activities and $75 million for awarding funds for activities promoting responsible fatherhood. The result was that the Title IV-A Healthy Marriage and Responsible Fatherhood programs, which were funded at $150 million annually[49] from FY2006 through FY2010, continued to be funded for an additional year (FY2011) on an equal basis.[50]

---

[49] As mentioned earlier, the healthy marriage grants were funded at about $100 million annually and the responsible fatherhood grant were funded at $50 million annually.

[50] Pursuant to P.L. 111-291, the $75 million in Responsible Fatherhood funds provided for FY2011 could be used for fatherhood activities intended to promote or sustain marriage, responsible parenting, economic stability, and media (continued...)

112th Congress (2011-2012)

The Obama Administration's FY2012 budget proposed continued funding of $150 million to support Healthy Marriages and Responsible Fatherhood programs for FY2012. These funds would have been split equally among Healthy Marriage and Responsible Fatherhood activities.

The Administration's FY2012 budget proposal also would have made changes to the purpose clause of the CSE program to include access and visitation and other fatherhood involvement activities. These activities would have become core parts of the CSE program and thereby states would have been reimbursed by the federal government for expenditures on such activities at an open-ended 66% matching rate. The budget proposal would have required states to establish access and visitation responsibilities in all initial child support orders. It would have encouraged states to undertake activities that support access and visitation, implementing domestic violence safeguards as a critical component of this new state responsibility. (The estimated cost of the proposal was $570 million over 10 years.)

The Obama Administration's FY2013 budget proposal was very similar to its FY2012 proposal with regard to responsible fatherhood programs.

During the 112th Congress, H.R. 2193, the Julia Carson Responsible Fatherhood and Healthy Families Act of 2011, was introduced on June 15, 2011, by Representative Danny Davis (et al.). Similar to the bill introduced in the 111th Congress, H.R. 2193, among other things, would have reauthorized and provided $75 million per year for responsible fatherhood programs for each of the years FY2011 through FY2015.

P.L. 112-78, the Temporary Payroll Tax Cut Continuation Act of 2011 (enacted December 23, 2011), provided funding for the Responsible Fatherhood Program (and the Healthy Marriage Program) through February 29, 2012. Thus, for the first five months of FY2012, the Healthy Marriage and Responsible Fatherhood grant programs were extended at their FY2011 funding level (i.e., $150 million per year on a pro rata basis, divided equally between the two programs).

P.L. 112-96, the Middle Class Tax Relief and Job Creation Act of 2012 (enacted February 22, 2012), provided funding for the Responsible Fatherhood Program (and the Healthy Marriage Program) through September 30, 2012 (i.e., through FY2012; at $150 million per year on a pro rata basis, divided equally between the two programs).

P.L. 112-175 (the government-wide continuing resolution enacted on September 28, 2012) extended funding for the Healthy Marriage and Responsible Fatherhood grant programs (at $150 million per year on a pro rata basis, divided equally between the two programs) through March 2013 (i.e., the first six months of FY2013).

(...continued)

campaigns that reach families with important messages about responsible fatherhood.

Author Contact Information

Carmen Solomon-Fears
Specialist in Social Policy
csolomonfears@crs.loc.gov, 7-7306

www.ingramcontent.com/pod-product-compliance
Lightning Source LLC
Chambersburg PA
CBHW080758290526
45790CB00008B/3501